Alex Asks About Auntie's Airplane Day

An Adoption Day Story

Carolyn Wilhelm

ILLUSTRATED BY PIETER ELS

Carolyn Wilhelm, Wise Owl Factory

9813 Zinnia Lane N

Maple Grove, MN 55369

https://www.thewiseowlfactory.com/

Some names and identifying details have been changed to protect the privacy of individuals. This is a work of fiction. Names, characters, places, and incidents are used factiously.

Book design © 2017, BookDesignTemplates.com

Cover design and all illustrations by illustrator Pieter Els

http://www.surferkiddies.com

(e) 978-0-9997766-0-5

(p) 978-0-9997766-1-2

US GOV Copyright TXu002081298

Printed in the United States of America

"Are we going to airplane day?" asked Alex.

"Yes," said mom.

1

"Will we fly in an airplane?" Alex asked.

"Not this time," said mom.

"Are we going to the airport?" Alex asked.

"Not this time," said dad.

"Look," said dad. "That is the hospital where you were born, Alex."

"I was a baby then, right?" asked Alex.

"Yes," said mom.

"Boom!" the tire exploded.

CLUNK! CLUNK! CLUNK!

The car went to the side of the road.

"What happened!" said Alex.

"Don't worry. It is just a flat tire. We will call grandpa," said dad.

"We will sit on the grass and wait," said mom.

"There is nothing to worry about."

"Won't we miss the party?" wondered a worried Alex.

"I'm here to help!" said grandpa.

"Oh, good," said Alex.

"I will get to see some tools!"

"Let's get the spare tire and the lug wrench out of the trunk," said grandpa.

Dad opened the trunk.

"What is a lug wrench?" Alex asked.

"This is a lug wrench," said grandpa.

"I'll help," said dad.

"I'm going to watch so I can learn how," said mom.

"Me, too," said Alex.

"See?" said grandpa.

"The lug wrench loosens the lug nuts so the tire can come off. Then it will tighten the lug nuts when we put on the new tire."

After thanking grandpa, Alex asked if they could still go to the party.

"Yes, we are on the way," said mom.

"Oh, look, there is an airplane party here," said dad.

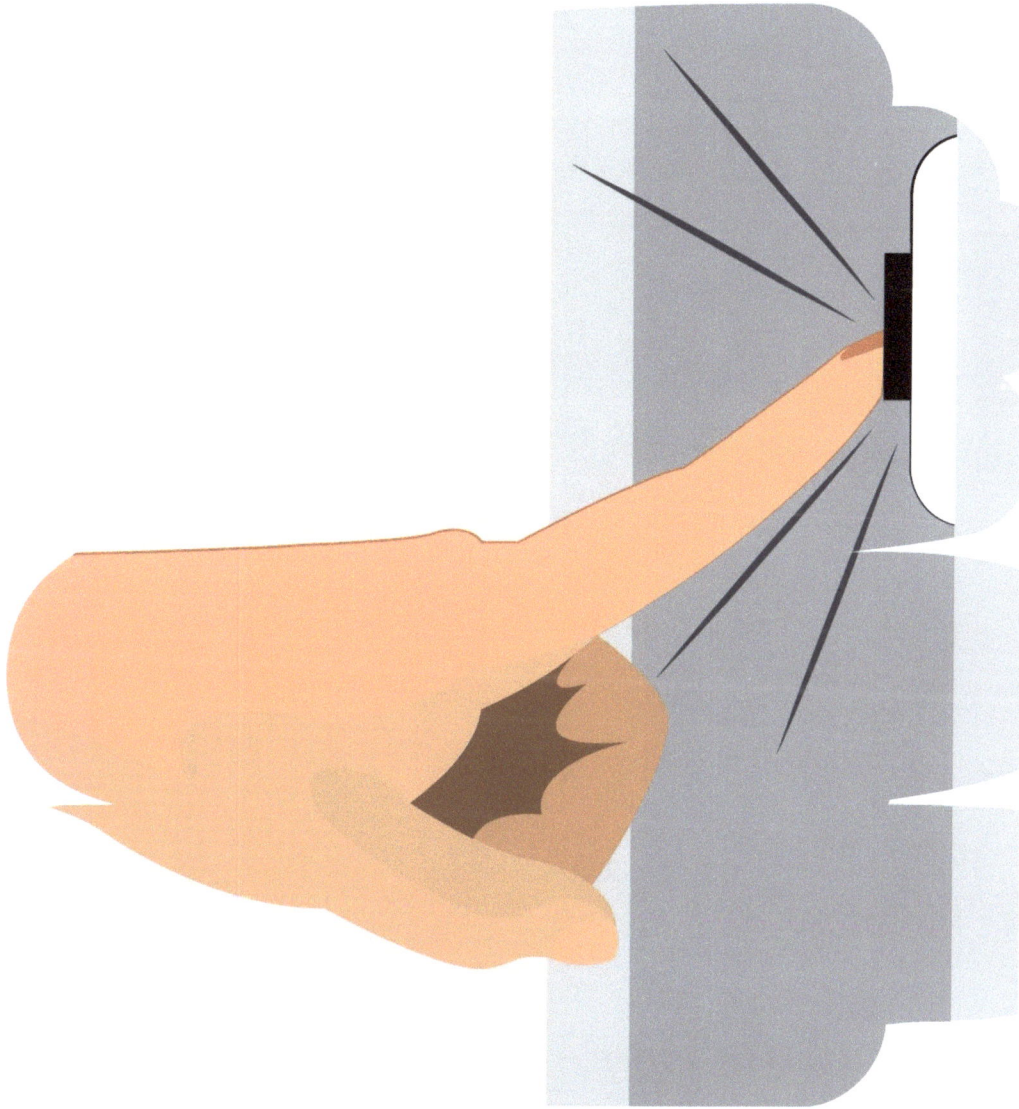

DING! DONG!

"Happy Airplane Day!" said mom, dad, and Alex.

"Thank you," said Auntie Betsy.

"Look! Grandpa is here with grandma," said
Alex.

"What is an airplane day?" Alex asked.

"We didn't go to the airport. We didn't ride an airplane. We didn't even see an airplane."

"Today is Auntie's airplane day as it is her adoption day. This was the date years ago when she arrived from South Korea on an airplane. So, we have an airplane theme party each year to celebrate the day," said grandpa.

"Wasn't she born in a hospital?" Alex asked.

"No, she was born at home and taken to a police station. That meant her mother wanted her to be adopted," answered mom.

"Then she went to stay with a foster family, until she could come to America," added grandma.

"It is different in different countries," said grandpa. "And it was many years ago."

"And I thought we had a difficult time getting here today with a flat tire," Alex realized.

"Adopted children are chosen and loved!" said grandma.

Auntie Betsy explained, "We call it *Airplane Day*. Some people call it *Adoption Day*. Some people call it *Gotcha Day*. But it is important to know adopted children grow up and still like to celebrate the special day with their families."

"Could we come back next year?" Alex asked.
"You are welcome anytime!" said Auntie
Betsy.

"Maybe we will see an airplane in the sky on the way home!" thought Alex.

"Maybe there will be a baby on it!"

"Let's not have another flat tire on the way home!" said dad.

"I'll help if you do," said grandpa.

"I think I could help this time," said mom.

"Me, too!" said Alex.

ABOUT THE AUTHOR

Carolyn Wilhelm has a BS in Elementary Education, an MS in Special Studies of Gifted Children, and an MA in Curriculum and Instruction K-12. She was a National Board Certification Middle Childhood Generalist 2004-2014. She is also a licensed, certified teacher in Minnesota through 2021. Previous publications include a story in the anthology *Mom for the Holidays: Stories of Love, Laughter & Tantrums at Christmas & Hanukkah* edited by Nolan and Demas. Carolyn is a wife, mom, and grandmother. One of her now adult children was adopted from South Korea. She is the author of the Wise Owl Factory which has (mostly) free educational materials for parents, teachers, homeschools, libraries, and scout groups to use. She lives with her witty and helpful husband of 47 years, and visits her children and grandchildren as often as she can.

Carolyn Wilhelm
Wise Owl Factory LLC
Minnesota
https://www.thewiseowlfactory.com/
@WiseOwlFactory.com

ABOUT THE ILLUSTRATOR

Pieter Els has 30+ years of experience in facilitating courses to junior and senior facilitators, learning aids development, course material development, and marketing and web design. At first, he has earned a Graphic Design Diploma and during his career, as well as several merit bonuses for outstanding educational services and products. Later in his career he decided to also get his BTech Degree in Graphic Design. Some of the other qualifications he obtained were: Educational Technology (EDTECH) Facilitator, Learning Aids Developer, Learning Material Developer and Assessor. He also took several courses in Computer Based Training, E-learning Software and attended Middle and Senior Management Courses. One of his major responsibilities later in his career was the research on distance learning.

Pieter has an online resource company for education clip art, illustrations, tutorials and articles. His company goal is to offer the world of education more high-quality art and learning materials. Surfer Kids Clip Art was established on Christmas Day, December 25, 2013
He is happily married to Elizabe with a daughter Nika and son Eswan.

Pieter Els
Surfer Kids Clip Art
Jeffreys Bay
South Africa
www.surferkiddies.com
surferkidsclipart@gmail.com

The idea for this book occurred to Carolyn when she saw her two-year-old grandson watch his Auntie Betsy from Korea and seem to wonder how she fit in the otherwise white family. Who knows what he was thinking, but it appeared to be he was noticing Auntie's eyes and skin color. Carolyn decided this book could help him and other young children with older, adopted relatives, understand a little about adoption.

Betsy spent her first ten months in ten different home placements in South Korea before being adopted through Children's Home Society in Minnesota. Once in Minnesota, she grabbed Carolyn and literally didn't let go, day or night, for about six months. She stayed near Carolyn for many years after the experience of having different caregivers prior to the final home placement. At first she didn't seem to be used to men, and wasn't immediately close to her new father. She learned to like him by the light of the digital clock, grabbing his mustache and finding out he was nice, little by little. We imagine the caretakers her first months were women. Apparently, the Korean practice of moving babies around too much has improved since 1980-81.

Don't tell Carolyn kids don't notice race! When her biological son was two (about the age when her grandson seemed to "notice" Betsy) he began to make comments. The most startling comment was that he was born from Carolyn's stomach, and Betsy was born from her back. Children are aware and perceptive and it is best to offer explanations appropriate to their age levels.

When Carolyn and Betsy go shopping or out to eat even today, they make comments to indicate to curious servers or cashiers that they are mother and daughter. It helps people who might not want to ask questions about their relationship. When the whole family is out together it seems to be less of an issue.

Families with different races have their own set of experiences and issues, and we would love to hear from you on this topic. We recommend the Multicultural Children's Book Day event in January of each year, as well as their blog for a variety of resources for families and teachers all year.
http://multiculturalchildrensbookday.com/

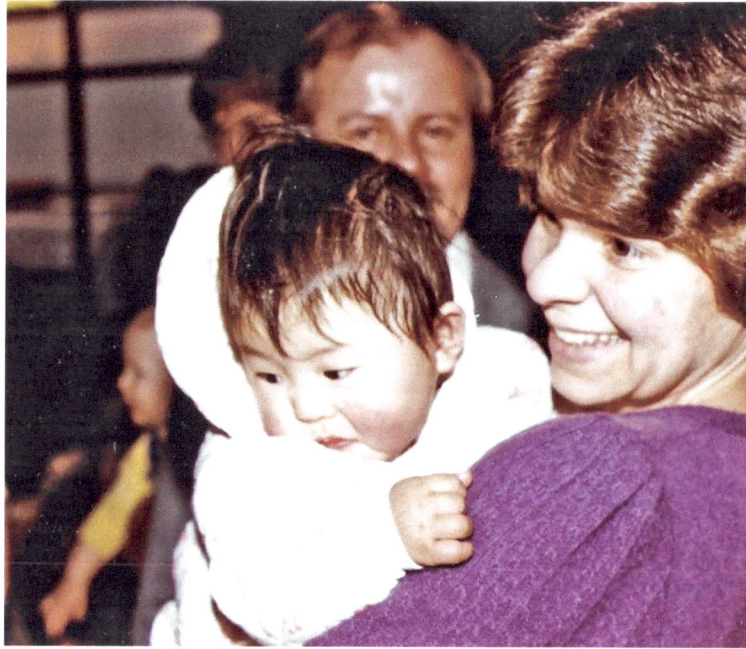

Betsy arrives at the Minneapolis airport from South Korea to the waiting arms of Carolyn, over 30 years ago.

You might also like Carolyn's blog post with free printable adoption day cards at Wise Owl Factory Alex Asks About Auntie's Airplane Day: An Adoption Story

Betsy and Carolyn have written a new book together. *A Mom: What is an Adoptive Mother?*

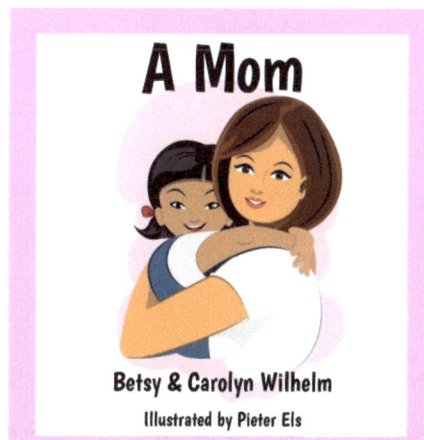

Discussion Points

1. What is "airplane day?"

2. What is adoption?

3. What is a foster family?

4. Compare and contrast Alex's travel to the airplane day celebration with Auntie's travel to her first airplane day.

5. Discuss why Alex might wonder about his Auntie's adoption.

6. There are many different kinds of families. What kinds of families do you know?

The idea with these discussion points is to help children become aware adults may have been adopted, not only babies. Children may realize adopted people have stories to share. Children may be familiar with flat tires or problems getting to an event, to compare with Auntie's travel as a baby to the USA. Children may be aware of multiracial families they know and perhaps share the names of such friends. Children may realize families are not all the same and can still be loving people. Children may come to realize that South Korea is a separate country from Japan and China through explanation (Asians are not all the same).

www.ingramcontent.com/pod-product-compliance
Lightning Source LLC
Chambersburg PA
CBHW042104040426
42448CB00002B/133